What Our Readers Have Said...

Applicability

"These books are great tools that should be used as guidelines for our everyday supervisory practices. You need to take the time to do a short self-evaluation when reading them."

•

"The things and problems we deal with everyday are discussed in these books."

•

Convenience

"I like this because I can take them with me to read at a convenient time. I feel the little time I have to spend in the office is best use on activities that directly relate to revenue opportunities. I like the short amount of time it takes to keep up with these."

•

"I just read each book, and then file it for future reference."

•

"I like the fact that the format allows the books to be reviewed as time permits. All work has been conducted on personal, evening/weekend time."

•

Challenge

"My thought is that the real value of these books comes into effect when doing the action plans."

•

"The challenge when I think a specific topic does not apply is to find a way to make it apply."

•

Clarity

"Short and sweet. These books are easy to comprehend."

•

"These books are very easy to read and clearly outlined."

•

"Easy to use, understand, and reference if needed."

•

Relevance

"I have enjoyed reading these books. They are relevant to today's work environment and the ongoing change in the way we manage our workforce."

•

"I believe the contents of the Pinpoint series are excellent. It causes one to reflect on the daily dynamics in working with oneself as well as with management and peers."

•

"I do feel that these books have been very helpful to me at my job."

•

"I do enjoy reading each of theses books and it gives some real thought to its instruction."

•

Improving Communication Skills

Pinpoint Customer Service Skill Development Training Series

TIMOTHY F. BEDNARZ

MAJORIUM
BUSINESS PRESS

Pinpoint Customer Service Skill Development Training Series
"Improving Communication Skills"
Timothy F. Bednarz

Graphic design: Monika Pawlak

Majorium Business Press
2025 Main Street
Stevens Point, WI 54481
715.342.1018 • 800.654.4935

ISBN 978-1-882181-40-7

Printed in the United States of America

Introduction

The Pinpoint Customer Service Skill Development Training Series is designed for targeted training and education regarding increased improvement in a specific skill or competency.

Each book within this series is designed to be easy to use, understand and apply to your job. It can be used as a basis for training individuals, as a discussion guide or as a personal training tool.

Each chapter within this book discusses a specific concept. When you have completed all eight chapters you should have a 360º perspective of the topic.

Additionally, each chapter is divided into specific sections:

- The first section provides you with an overview of the topic
- The Implications section discusses why the concept is important, and why it is important to learn and apply.
- The Strategies, Tips & Techniques to Apply section teaches how to use and apply the particular concept to your work.
- The Points to Ponder section gives you something to think about or to be discussed with a group setting. These are questions not meant to be immediately answered, but to be pondered over time.
- The Training Activity section provides you with the tools to transfer what you have learned to your job. It is designed to help create an action plan to effectively apply the concept.

Each of the topics in this series is time-tested and proven in the marketplace. They have been used by thousands of employees as training tools. Many of the users have commented that what made these books valuable, was the ability to refer to them when a problem surfaced. They indicated that they remembered reading about the exact problem. They referred back to these books and found an appropriate solution.

You will find them equally valuable as a resource in your professional development library.

Table of Contents

LEARNING OBJECTIVES:

- To understand the purpose of good communication.
- To effectively use communication.
- To apply effective communication techniques.
- To use various communication techniques to transmit an effective message.
- To obtain results through the effective use of communication.

1

How Customers Judge Your Communication Style

Customer service communication is based upon mastering correct applications and procedures for transferring ideas, thoughts and messages to customers in all types of situations. Professional service representatives communicate through learned responses and repeated methods that have worked well in former experiences. This is because they generally have awarded more positive outcomes than negative ones. However, this does not imply that all responses have positive effects associated with them. The combination of using successful communication methods helps to create service representatives' professional personal styles, or, in other words, their "image."

All customer service representatives present a certain communication image to their customers. This communication image mirrors not only their personality and style, but also creates an opinion about the particular way problems will be resolved and about the various products or services that are represented in terms of quality and value. That is why often it becomes necessary to reflect upon one's personal communication strengths and weaknesses. The influence it has creates a direct impact on all customers and the encounters with them.

IMPLICATIONS – WHAT THIS MEANS TO YOU

Customer service representatives must incorporate and maintain a good communication image style, using it as a significant part of meeting their customers' needs, solving their problems, and motivating them to maintain their company loyalty. Personal communication strength comes from the inward desire and commitment to communicate thoughts, messages, ideas and knowledge as effectively as possible. It often means fighting verbal laziness and shortcuts when communicating.

Customers who stand on the other side of the counter, opposite sides of the order blank, or at the customer service desk, have only one way to judge the individuals and companies they deal with: through a combination of visible actions and verbal interactions. It is imperative harmony exists between the two, for it can make the difference between having customers interpret positive messages of honesty, trustworthiness and feelings of importance, or to translate them as "you and your company don't care" negative ones.

STRATEGIES, TIPS & TECHNIQUES TO APPLY

Communication between customers and service representatives revolves around four basic components. These basic elements of conversation lead toward customer satisfaction or hostility, depending upon one's mastery over them. The four components are: the message, the customer service person, the customer and the situation. Service representatives' professional communication images become apparent once they begin to interrelate with their customers. They are generally unaware that customers automatically begin to dissect personalities and characteristics, which are the basis for interpreting and forming opinions as to whether or not positive communication styles exist. In other words, customers react accordingly to every customer service representative's individual image.

Generally all professional service people possess the ability to speak fluently and communicate relatively well without even thinking about it. Yet there are times they can easily stumble, when particular circumstances catch them off guard. For some unknown reason, "verbal fatigue" emerges. Something happens between the link of mind and speech, and service representatives begin to project themselves verbally into something other than what they really are. They stammer, searching for the right word or phrase, struggling with facial grimaces and frowns as the customer stands there observing, weighing, and judging their overall performance or their communication image. All individuals possess very different communication styles and skills. These set service representatives apart from one another as uniquely as their personalities do.

The primary aim of every conversation is to create a comfortable atmosphere for customers to function within. The second priority is to establish message credibility. No matter what basic communication type or combination is displayed, customer service representatives should always move in these two directions. In each conversation the key is to counterbalance effectiveness. Taking responsibility to keep the channels of good communication open is vital to create a polished image.

There are 14 tips that may help overcome or prevent negative conversational habits when dealing with customers. These references may prove useful to maintain a highly polished communication image.

1. Keep emotions out of the customer service process and conversations.
2. Stay focused on each particular customer's concerns, problems or solutions.
3. Seek to ascertain your customers' needs.
4. Be persistent in establishing a positive conversational climate.
5. When you find yourself at the receiving end of a hostile or negative conversation, stand firm, but maintain a positive stature.
6. Get back on track to the causes and concerns quickly if customers steer you off course.
7. Smile, using fluid movements as you converse with your customers.
8. Be polite, but be sure to ask customers to rephrase facts, key points, or ideas if they are unclear.
9. Tell your customers they are important to you and your company. Do it sincerely.
10. Tell customers you will always be available, if and when they need you.
11. Show more and tell less.
12. Say only what you mean.

13. Always leave your customer encounters with a kind word.

14. Let your first communication priority be to win the respect of your customers and to earn their appreciation.

A good communication style creates the raw material for opportunity. It is necessary to get customers to the point of feeling they are totally satisfied with the process and outcomes. Individual communication styles should be linked with directness and openness in order to cement their loyalty. Displaying caring and concern is necessary, but it is easy to carry it to the point of becoming unbelievable.

Changing communication styles can begin with adapting or modifying current ones that are used. Remaining fluid and flexible in various styles and patterns of communication is essential. Working on the weaknesses can make a big difference in how customers react. Great opportunities are generally the result of wise improvements made upon small details.

POINTS TO PONDER — SOMETHING TO THINK ABOUT

1. How effectively are you able to communicate your thoughts and messages? How realistic is your self-assessment? Explain.
2. Where do you feel some of your communication problems stem?

TRAINING ACTIVITY — APPLICATION & ACTION PLAN

Decide what your current communication image is, as your customers interpret it.

1. Analyze areas of strengths and weaknesses in how you communicate that projects the image you feel others have of you.
2. Determine ways to overcome communication weaknesses in order to polish up your "image".

2

The Implications of Effective Communication

The implications of effective communication can be measured at every stage of the service encounter process. How techniques are applied can greatly help or hinder customer service reps in the performance of their jobs and in gaining the satisfaction from their positions, which ultimately determines their overall solution seeking abilities and customer loyalty success.

Until customer service reps are able to develop the necessary skills to become totally masterful professional communicators, they can expect to experience frustration and added anxiety as well as unhappy customers in terms of the solutions offered to them. Effective communication skills are the foundation for successful service encounters.

IMPLICATIONS — WHAT THIS MEANS TO YOU

Many customer service reps define communication by how well they speak or write, but it goes far beyond these two elements. Effective communication is the ability to totally identify a problem, issue or need, clearly understand it, design a solution and effectively communicate it back to the customer in a persuasive way.

Ineffective communication methods have specific implications and ramifications that ultimately affect all customer service reps. This is important to consider because without the masterful ability to effectively communicate to customers, they are severely hampered in their personal abilities to sell their concepts, ideas and solutions. Effective communication is an essential and critical tool all service reps must possess and apply.

STRATEGIES, TIPS & TECHNIQUES TO APPLY

Most customer service reps don't analyze the impact of effective communication. Consider the following implications:

Shapes Initial Impressions

Those who do not possess effective communication skills have difficulty making a good initial impression and therefore fall short in making customers feel comfortable when they want to open up and discuss their problems in a rational way. It often hinders service reps from being able to match proper solutions to exact needs and wants.

Customer service reps have generally less than 30 seconds to define and cement into their customers' minds, one or two compelling reasons why they should provide any additional input to take the service process further. Successful ones can communicate explicit reasons quickly and effectively.

Gains Access to Customers

Customer service reps that do not possess the skill or ability to clearly demonstrate their professional expertise will not often be given a second chance to do so. Customers are much too busy and overly stressed to educate them about their problems, issues or concerns more than once without becoming upset. If customer service reps cannot effectively communicate a distinct solution advantage quickly and effectively, calls will be cut short and problems will become more difficult to resolve.

Communicates Benefits

Without effective communication skills customer service reps are not able to effectively uncover hidden agendas, implications and intended messages.

Without this knowledge, they become further ineffective in communicating their own solution benefits and how they are able to positively impact and alleviate their customers' worries and concerns.

Differentiates Products or Services

Customer service reps must be able to understand and communicate the key differences between their products and services and those of the competition. Unless they possess the right persuasive words and phrases, they will not be able to design and implement effective solution outcomes that build and sustain their customers' loyalty, keeping them out of the hands of the competition.

Advances the Service Process Forward

Customer service reps must use effective communication skills clearly and concisely to smoothly advance the service encounter. If they cannot effectively listen, question, identify problems and concerns, clarify issues, craft solutions and put them into positive action for their customers, it becomes impossible to move them toward a commitment of solution acceptance.

Avoids Creating Service Barriers

Customer service reps must be able to effectively communicate to adequately qualify their customers' problems, their related issues, ramifications and long-term impacts in order to comprehend their levels of priority and concern. A failure to qualify and categorize potential problems results in presenting particular solutions that customers have little interest in pursuing. The improper problem or issue qualification process is the primary cause of barriers to the acceptance of specific service solutions. All are effects of faulty or inappropriate communication.

Shapes Perceptions and Defines Expectations

Customer service reps who fail to manage and control the perceptions they create and the resulting expectations, can expect to experience multiple problems once the initial service encounter comes to a close. They need to effectively and carefully communicate their thoughts and messages to develop and shape proper perceptions, and to define accurate and realistic expectations in regard to possible solution alternatives.

Communicates and Delivers Value

Value is defined as repeatedly meeting or exceeding customers' expectations. If customer service reps are lax in accurately and precisely defining solution expectations or are careless in how they communicate their messages, they will be unable to effectively sell their solution's value and successfully reinforce it.

POINTS TO PONDER — SOMETHING TO THINK ABOUT

1. How carefully do you manage your communication with your customers?
2. Have you experienced problems and ramifications because of possibly communicating your thoughts and messages ineffectively?

TRAINING ACTIVITY — APPLICATION & ACTION PLAN

1. Perform a personal communication's evaluation. List on a sheet of paper the following factors. Next to each, rate yourself as highly effective, effective, fairly effective or not effective.
    - Shapes Initial Impressions
    - Gains Access to Customers
    - Communicates Service Benefits
    - Differentiation
    - Advances the Service Encounter
    - Avoids Creating Service Barriers

- Shapes Perceptions and Defines Expectations
- Communicates and Delivers Value

2. Based upon your responses, determine the areas where you need to improve upon. Identify the reasons why you feel you are ineffective and determine exactly how you can improve in the specific areas selected. List several suggestions of what can be done to increase your communication effectiveness.

3

Overcoming the Primary Barrier of Effective Communication

The primary barrier to mutual communication often comes from a natural tendency to judge, evaluate, approve or disapprove what is being directly communicated. This occurs because most customer service reps tend to evaluate what they hear from their own personal points of view and frames of reference, which short-circuits the process to think, reframe and analyze responses effectively.

IMPLICATIONS – WHAT THIS MEANS TO YOU

Customer service reps must not only be able to communicate their own thoughts, ideas, and messages effectively, but they are also responsible for facilitating better communication between customers that have divergent and often opposing points of view.

Customer service reps must understand that communication is heightened when personal feelings and emotions are deeply involved. One rule of thumb always applies: the stronger the personal feelings of the involved parties, the less likely there will be any mutual elements between the two. This is because two ideas, two sets of personal feelings and two sets of judgments exist, which are completely disconnected. When this occurs, nothing remotely resembling communication takes place.

This is important for customer service reps to seriously think about, because they are often placed in situations and circumstances where there is a complete lack of communication occurring during service encounters. They can be placed in the middle of a situation where communication completely breaks down due to the emotional content of the argument. Without an understanding of the factors that directly affect communication, customer service reps will find themselves undermined and unable to facilitate or maintain effective two-way communication. The process subsequently ends up producing aggravation, conflict and frustration for both parties involved.

STRATEGIES, TIPS & TECHNIQUES TO APPLY

Actual communication occurs and personal evaluations are avoided when customer service reps listen with a sense of understanding. This becomes a direct result of comprehending an expressed idea or attitude from the other person's point of view and developing an inward sense of how the other individual feels. Doing this allows them to achieve a personal frame of reference linked directly to the other individual's thoughts, perceptions and mental interpretations. When customer service reps are able to develop this understanding, they are better able to facilitate open communication, alter and modify the other party's fears, and establish more realistic and harmonious relationships with their customers.

Customer service reps can effectively apply this technique in a difficult communication environment by requiring customers involved in a verbal conflict to accurately restate their opinions, ideas and feelings. Only after this is accomplished are customer service reps free to state their own viewpoints in response.

This should be done each time customers wish to state their viewpoints or make particular verbal statements or responses. The reason this technique is so effective is because it forces customers to pause and consider their points of reference, which helps to identify what lies beneath their thought processes. This technique works because it immediately gives both individuals time to pause, think, analyze, evaluate, and remove the emotion from their statements.

This technique requires one individual to achieve the other's frame of reference, understanding his or her thoughts and feelings well enough to summarize them accurately. This establishes real two-way communication that guarantees that reasonable solutions can be obtained. It accomplishes this for two major reasons. When understanding is achieved, it forces one or both parties to revise personal statements and alterations in thinking while removing damaging emotions. Additionally, it reduces the differences between conflicting individuals while making viewpoints, opinions and thoughts rational and understandable to deal with.

Customer service reps should be advised that complete discussion understanding is often difficult to achieve because of the risks associated with challenging individual thinking processes, which includes the necessary capability of altering another person's point of view. Most individuals are afraid of this personal risk.

Additionally, when emotions are at their peak, it is extremely difficult to achieve another's frame of reference at the exact point where it is needed most to effectively interpret what is actually being said.

Customer service reps can easily overcome this barrier by taking the role of acting as a neutral third party. In this capacity, they restate each position and point of reference to build clarity, introspection and understanding. This is an effective method for neutralizing potential miscommunication problems through proactive personal interaction. When customers realize they are being understood clearly and accurately, and they feel comfortable because their views are being mirrored, their statements grow less exaggerated and less defensive.

Taking the position of a neutral third party allows customer service reps to handle any insincerities, exaggerations, lies and "false fronts" that typically characterize almost every customer communication breakdown. This method leads to the discovery of the truth and a realistic objective appraisal of the barriers that are occurring to inhibit two-way interactive communication. The aim is to achieve mutual communication, which focuses upon solving problems rather than attacking customers' ideas, methods of reasoning or appraisals.

POINTS TO PONDER — SOMETHING TO THINK ABOUT

1. What have you found to be a barrier to your personal communication?
2. Do you find yourself guilty of evaluating a customer's statements without fully understanding his or her point of view?

TRAINING ACTIVITY — APPLICATION & ACTION PLAN

When dealing with a communication problem, require the customer involved to restate his or her opinions, ideas and feelings accurately to your satisfaction. Then state your particular viewpoints.

This should be done each time customers wish to state their viewpoints or make a statement in response to your comments or questions.

If the customers involved are unable to do this effectively, act as a neutral third-party, stating each position precisely and carefully throughout the critical steps of the discussion process.

4

Negative Communication Styles Tarnish Your Image

Service communication is based upon accurately applying the right techniques for transferring thoughts and messages directly to customers throughout the various phases of the service encounter. The combination of effectively using the most successful methods for communicating various messages creates a positive service "image." A negative communication style tarnishes this professional image.

IMPLICATIONS – WHAT THIS MEANS TO YOU

All customer service reps possess the ability to speak fluently and communicate relatively well. Yet there are times, especially when a particular issue or circumstance catches them off-guard, where they begin to stumble. When this occurs, customer service reps often resort to using one or more of three negative communication styles.

This is important to consider because when placed into a stressful situation, there is a tendency to assume a defensive and negative communication style. Often this is done unconsciously, but the results can be detrimental to the health of particular service outcomes. This is because customers tend to observe, weigh and judge customer service reps' overall communication performance, which is how their image is defined and perceived.

STRATEGIES, TIPS & TECHNIQUES TO APPLY

Customer service reps must maintain an effective communication image and style as a tool to meet their customers' needs and solve their problems and concerns. More importantly, effective communication must move customers continually forward toward satisfaction. Negative communication styles interfere with this process.

There are three basic negative communication styles that may mirror customer service reps' personal traits. Addressing each improves overall communication with customers.

The 'I'm Sorry' Style

With the "I'm sorry" style, customer service reps are continually apologetic about their words and actions. It is often seen in those who have a need to seek approval from others. At its most extreme, this style focuses on customers' interpretations and judgments at the expense of the service focus and imparted messages. It often negatively affects the message's information and clarity. It negatively affects a professional communication image when numerous apologies, overdone explanations and repeated phrases and sentences are consistently offered.

Rather than giving themselves time to think, customer service reps will tend to use fillers during pauses and get carried away on tangents that cause them to lose their conversational focus and direction. Consequently, customers begin to question their credibility.

However, there is a positive side to this style. Customer service reps generally only exhibit a few of these characteristics. Most of the time, people who fall into this style tend to compensate. They generally excel in nonverbal communication using smiles, displaying friendly eyes and positive nods. The most undesirable habits can be easily diminished through confidence and assertiveness building.

The Commanding Style

The "commanding" style of communication is where customer service reps tend to dominate conversations. Those who use this style generally display perfect control over their conversations. They are polished communicators, except they have a tendency to focus on themselves and not on their customers. The use of their words and phrases displays high levels of energy, yet, at the same time, suggests to their customers that they unconditionally deserve the right to impart their knowledge and opinions even if they are not solicited.

Customers can react positively or negatively to this style, depending upon their own methods of communicating. Customer service reps using the commanding style often lack the time and patience to listen for details and reasons. Their phrases, tone and inflections often carry an attitude that suggests little concern about what customers think. Consequently, communicated messages often leave them with a feeling of total dissatisfaction in regard to the whole service process. Customers begin to feel that what is being said is not totally believable. Because of it, their business is often lost even if a solution outcome is satisfactory.

The positive side of this style is that customer service reps are generally exceptionally articulate, well organized and creative. They are able to use their infallible memory for imparting facts and details in a concerned manner and use open-ended questions to their fullest advantage. This brings their customers' perspectives into the open regarding problems, situations and solutions.

Customer service reps that habitually fall into the commanding style often forget it is easier to analyze situations when they take the time to slow down. It often becomes necessary for them to work on and improve their active listening skills.

The Machine Style

The "machine" style is when customer service reps communicate too much, and listen too little. Those who fall into this style of communicating generally exhibit strength in problem solving and developing effective solutions because of their tendency to be factual. Additionally, these customer service reps tend to continually use silence. They find this style comfortable because it provides a functional wall to fend off emotional threats.

This mode of communication can easily create negative interference within the service process. Some customers react to longer pauses and silence as a sign of hostility.

These customer service reps are prone to creating tension within their service encounters. When using this style, they are not aware of nor do they incorporate thinking and talking speeds that allow customers to understand better. This creates an outward appearance of insensitivity on their part, especially concerning a customer's time constraint and specific concerns. This in turn produces impatience on the customer's part.

Messages from the machine communicator are strong in content and ideas, but are for the most part emotionally weak. To overcome a depersonalized service message, it is important to develop insights that offer greater in-depth understanding of each customer's needs, wants, cares and concerns.

The best way for customer service reps to overcome the machine style of communicating is to be more aware of how they evaluate a situation and assess the information heard throughout the service process, and not after all the input has been gathered and discussed. They can turn this negative style into a positive one when they use their strengths to help struggling customers prioritize issues, concerns and problems. This is extremely important when specific problems surface that are more complex in nature or when multiple factors need to be addressed in order to solve a detailed, interwoven or complex problem.

POINTS TO PONDER — SOMETHING TO THINK ABOUT

1. Do you have a tendency to alter your communication style when placed into a stressful situation by a customer?
2. Can you think of any specific situations when these personal communication tendencies possibly harmed the service process or encounter?

TRAINING ACTIVITY — APPLICATION & ACTION PLAN

1. Perform a self-analysis of your communication style. On a sheet of paper list the three styles:
    - I'm Sorry
    - Commanding
    - Machine
2. Ask yourself the following questions and rate your responses on a scale of 1 to 10, with ten having the most negative impact as far as personal tendencies.
    - Do I often tend to apologize for my words or actions?
    - Do I tend to dominate the conversation with my customers?
    - Do I tend to present too much information and listen too little?

    A higher score indicates a strong tendency to use a specific negative style. It indicates the need to address it.
3. Modify your communication behavior with the suggestions offered. Add additional suggestions to the list. Work to reduce specific negative communication factors. Take your strengths and build upon them.

5

The Causes of Communication Breakdowns

Many customer service reps often demonstrate individual behaviors and attitudes that unwittingly impact their communication in a negative way. Their efforts end up repelling customers or prospects rather than attracting them. The ramifications include lost sales, lost customers, and the inability to build and sustain long-term customer relationships. Consequences are seen in frustrations and personal anxieties that surface from a persistent sense of failure and a general feeling of inadequacy. Customer service reps affected by this end up wallowing in confusion, finding it difficult to understand and explain the causes of their communication breakdowns.

IMPLICATIONS — WHAT THIS MEANS TO YOU

There are many reasons why communication disintegrates. Many breakdowns deal with personal issues, or the emotional baggage customer service reps bring to the job. Fortunately, once they are able to identify the causes of communication problems, they can start to work to resolve these particular issues to increase their overall effectiveness.

Identifying the causes of communication breakdown is an important first step. Most of these problems are the result of learned behaviors that with careful and immediate attention can be remedied. However, if left unchecked these become barriers that will continue to produce persistent failure and hinder the ability of customer service reps to reach their full potential.

STRATEGIES, TIPS & TECHNIQUES TO APPLY

Customer service reps can be easily tripped up when they communicate. A number of factors can affect what they say or bias their conversations in such a way as to make the sales message weak or off-focus. These factors include:

Fears

Most fears are learned. They are rooted in past experiences or from learned biases. Many stem from a deep-seated lack of self-esteem or diminished personal confidence in one's ability to perform adequately and professionally. Many customer service reps have personal fears of not being able to meet their prospects' expectations. Because of it they get flustered, becoming intimidated and fearful that they might say the wrong thing or make a statement that makes them appear to be ignorant or unprofessional. When customer service reps become fearful, their ability to communicate is greatly impaired. Rather than be made to look foolish or be misinterpreted, they closely control and guard their communication, which makes them appear to be more sheepish rather than assertive when attempting to gather the information they need to effectively sell.

Assumptions

While many assumptions made by customer service reps may be initially correct, communication breaks down when they accept and firmly believe their assumptions. When this happens there is a tendency to sell from what they think is accurate and reliable knowledge and information. They disregard questioning and clarifying facts, issues and data.

When customer service reps listen to their prospects, it is natural for them to make assumptions. They immediately take shape when they begin to interpret every word, gesture, inflection and tone. However, some of their assumptions may be inaccurate. Meanings may be derived that are not intended or implied. The communication process breaks down because customer service reps think a specific message is communicated when in fact a particular prospect is saying and thinking something completely different. The key to preventing a communication breakdown from unwarranted or misinterpreted assumptions is to make certain the verbal message is clearly understood in the same way by both parties involved.

Insensitivity

Communication can breakdown when there is a failure to accurately perceive the needs, feelings and concerns of others. The problem frequently occurs when customer service reps ignore their prospects' stated needs and concerns and proceed to present a product or service that does not specifically address these two issues. It ultimately becomes one that is of no interest to potential buyers.

Labeling

Often without a comprehensive understanding of prospects businesses, needs, potential size and their ability to make a purchase, some customer service reps begin to subconsciously label them. Perhaps a particular facility or a prospect's personal appearance makes a poor initial impression. Automatically, customer service reps can easily begin to categorize them. Once this occurs a bias is formed that can significantly reduce the sales opportunity that certain prospects can actually provide. Conversations and comments often reflect inward negative impressions and interpretations.

Uncertainty

Ineffective speaking habits or patterns that instill a sense and feeling of uncertainty in sales conversations surface from customer service reps' individual fears, mental laziness or a conviction that they are incapable of presenting valid and acceptable pictures and perspectives in regard to their particular products or services. This uncertainty often results in extremely long pauses of silence, which subsequently produce increased stress levels and a feeling of intimidation. Under these circumstances, customer service reps cannot either speak or listen effectively, which actively taints the relationship-building and communication process.

Resentment

Resentment is a level of personal bitterness that has the ability to destroy sales careers as well as potential business relationships. Customer service reps can often become resentful of a particular prospect's position, status or income. The source of this resentment may be from the fact that they presently feel they are not working for a more prestigious company. Feelings of resentment fester to the point where reps begin to continually look for the worst in people and situations. Unfortunately, their conversations, tone and implications reflect it. This practice taints personal viewpoints and perspectives throughout the sales communication process. Everything they say or do becomes biased and distorted. Consequently, prospects become repelled and emotional.

Egotism

While customer service reps require a healthy ego in order to be successful in a profession wrought with failure and rejection, an ego too strong conveys a lack of respect and interest. Personal egos can hinder the ability to properly identify important needs and concerns. A strong ego is seen when customer service reps dominate their sales conversations without allowing their prospects to provide in-depth input and feedback. The consequence is seen in poor sales, numerous objections, stalls, barriers, and poor customer retention. Customer service reps with strong egos are incapable of building solid and sustainable relationships.

POINTS TO PONDER — SOMETHING TO THINK ABOUT

1. Have you experienced problems and barriers to your success that could possibly be attributed to any of the above listed causes of communication breakdowns?
2. Do you have a sense that something has been holding you back in your sales relationships and closings, but find yourself unable to pinpoint exactly what the problem is?

TRAINING ACTIVITY — APPLICATION & ACTION PLAN

Perform a personal self-evaluation of your communication skills.

1. Identify any causes of breakdowns.
2. Review the following list of causes and determine if any of them apply to you.
    - Fears
    - Assumptions
    - Insensitivity
    - Labeling
    - Uncertainty
    - Resentment
    - Egotism
3. Once you are aware of what problems may be occurring, assess what you think creates a particular problem and what actions you need to take to rectify it.

6

Developing Positive Communication's Traits

When it comes to communicating effectively, the first thought many customer service reps have is that they must be eloquent and intelligent in how they say and present their messages. Individuals who worry about displaying their professional eloquence immediately begin to focus on *how* something is being communicated, rather than on *what* is being imparted. It is the old argument of form over substance. However, it is the personalities and attitudes of customer service reps that actually help or hinder their communication.

IMPLICATIONS – WHAT THIS MEANS TO YOU

The success of service communication depends to a large degree upon service reps' personality traits. As was explained in an earlier lesson, many communication breakdowns are created by personal problems, attitudes and conflicts that customer service reps bring to their job. Once they understand what is causing communication breakdowns and failures, they can take the necessary steps to modify or alter them. However, there are positive personality traits that do facilitate effective communication.

This is important for customer service reps to consider because when they understand the traits that can best help their communications, they can learn to skillfully manage and apply them. When they understand the negative ones, they are able to work to effectively eliminate them. Most individuals go through life without ever understanding how these traits have the ability to alter their lives in either a positive or negative way.

STRATEGIES, TIPS & TECHNIQUES TO APPLY

Since effective communication is a personal issue, it stands to reason there are positive communication traits customer service reps can develop and skillfully apply, including:

Self-Awareness

Self-awareness is a personal understanding of one's attitudes and convictions, how they were formed and how they can be adapted and modified to maximize individual performance. It helps customer service reps to understand their personal values and beliefs as well as a strong self-commitment that these are worth sharing with others.

Some customer service reps may not consider self-awareness to be an important trait or one that makes any difference in relationship to the service environment. However, it is the core beliefs, attitudes and convictions that internally motivate customer service reps and shape how they will serve or treat a customer.

Understanding

Before customer service reps can effectively serve their customers, they must have the personal desire to fully understand their needs, concerns, worries, fears and problems. While this may seem elementary on the surface, the truth is many do not possess this desire. They have only the inclination to get through the encounter and move on. There is little or no concern displayed for their customers' feelings, fears, satisfaction or consequences.

Successful customer service reps have an internal desire to fully understand their customers' problems and issues and to grasp the ramifications solutions have on their business and personal life. They communicate this desire with the use of effective questioning techniques to probe for hidden needs, complex interrelated issues and major related concerns. Additionally, they question all of their own assumptions and clarify customers' statements and expectations to avoid any miscommunication or misinterpretation.

Care and Concern

When customer service reps focus on their personal needs, their motivation becomes transparent. Customers soon know they are not a top priority. Because of it, they quickly stop listening and interacting.

Customer service reps may wonder how customers can sense this. It is because their words, actions, gestures and facial expressions clearly transmit the message even if there are attempts to mask it. Individuals can sense genuine concern and empathy. When customer service reps are warm, interesting, and caring, they automatically open the door to effective communication and instill a sense of believability and trustworthiness.

Emotional Control

Customer service reps have the ability to control their personal emotions. Once they understand that anger, bitterness and hostility produce no positive effects and, in reality, prevent them from achieving their goals, they are in a position to alter their choice of behaviors and actions.

Customer service reps often become victims of frustration, depression, envy, resentment, anger and jealousy. They also have a choice to develop the internal fortitude needed to rise above these feelings. Negative emotions do not have a place in their professional career and only serve to hinder growth, productivity, effectiveness and personal happiness. Fully understanding this, customer service reps who are boxed in by their emotions can motivate themselves to change.

Self-Esteem

A healthy self-esteem is a key element that all customer service reps need to possess. It is the personal inward strength that allows them to overcome the continuous frustrations and anxieties associated with the service profession as a whole.

A low self-esteem is the consequence of accepting someone else's standard for their own personal self-worth. Often these types of individuals tend to judge others on superficial values, such as from the viewpoint of beauty, money or popularity.

All individuals are unique and endowed with their own skills and talents. Developing and maintaining a healthy self-esteem comes from the ability to recognize them and to use them to their fullest while avoiding attempts to meet another person's expectations.

Self-Confidence

Self-confidence is based upon one's personal level of self-esteem. It means individuals can trust and rely on their personal resources and judgment in any given situation. Total self-confidence allows customer service reps to take the necessary risks head on to be successful in meeting new situations while confidently servicing their customers without fear.

Sharing

In order to provide excellent service and to build good relationships, customer service reps must be willing to give and share ideas, feelings and perspectives. This also means sharing a personal commitment to their customers' success and the expertise and experience to ensure complete satisfaction. Successful customer service means that customer service reps must be able to give generously of themselves in order to build and sustain solid relationships, knowing full well that if their customers are satisfied, their own personal needs will be met.

POINTS TO PONDER — SOMETHING TO THINK ABOUT

1. Are you aware of any positive or negative communication patterns and/or traits you personally use on a consistent basis?
2. Have you been able to identify any positive communication traits you were not previously aware of? Are there ones you never associated as being important for effective service communications?

TRAINING ACTIVITY — APPLICATION & ACTION PLAN

Many customer service reps express negative communication patterns without being aware of them.

1. For the next week, develop extensive notes about your conversations.
2. Write them down or tape-record them.
3. Analyze your communication habits and patterns for negative influences or effects.
4. Create several suggestions to help overcome some of the negative traits, if any exist.

7

Personal Communication Skills

Personal communication skills go beyond the ability to write a letter, send emails or make an effective point. A powerful interactive communication process is the overall ability to communicate using verbal as well as nonverbal techniques. It is having the capacity to become attuned to customers by sensing beyond words exactly what they are saying and implying.

IMPLICATIONS – WHAT THIS MEANS TO YOU

Customer service reps may have the knowledge of effective communication techniques, but it is the application of them that is important to become successful in their profession. They must be totally professional communicators. Without this, the other essential skills required to identify needs and present valid solutions become ineffective. The ability to personally communicate well in all situations has far-reaching implications and ramifications.

This is important because effective communicators will accomplish far more, even if they lack expertise and knowledge, compared to customer service reps that display high levels of expertise and knowledge but lack effective interactive communication skills. Those who wish to reach the pinnacle of their profession must master all forms of communication and possess the ability to effectively use each with their customers, associates, superiors and friends.

STRATEGIES, TIPS & TECHNIQUES TO APPLY

Effective communication makes things happen. It breaks down resistance barriers, opens doors, allows people to vent their frustrations and helps to build solid bridges. Good communication provides customer service reps with the ability to discuss difficult issues and motivate their customers into action.

The development of effective communication skills is continuous. It is an honest and sincere attempt to share ideals, vision, thoughts, interests and concepts. This in turn allows individuals to discover what they have in common with one another. It is an essential element of relationship building.

The more customer service reps know about their customers, the stronger their ability becomes to build and sustain long-term relationships with them. Good communication skills build trust and credibility that become the essential foundational structure for business relationships.

The underlying rule in communication is to have enthusiasm and confidence to serve customers successfully. Customer service reps can make communications work to their benefit by using the following techniques each day.

- **Smile and really mean it.** A warm and genuine smile communicates more to customers than anything else. Additionally, a warm smile compels customer service reps to open up their body language so that it corresponds with their smiles.
- **Bring communication into the personal realm.** Customer service reps should get customers to open up by asking about their personal interests and viewpoints. It is important to get them to talk about themselves, including their personal goals and items of concern and importance.
- **Ask if there is a better time to discuss issues** if customers appear to be busy and stressed. This communicates a strong sense of caring, concern and respect for their time and emotions. There is more to gain than lose with this technique. If customers are not focused on a discussion, the time spent will be ineffective. It is vital to have their undivided attention.
- **Vary the speed of speech**, allowing space and pauses between thoughts

and sentences. This makes customer service reps' verbal communications more interesting and easier to listen to. Dull and monotone speech patterns can be boring and negatively interfere with the message.

- **Focus on one subject at a time**, allowing customers to ask questions or voice their opinions. This allows for a full examination of a specific topic that can uncover other issues.
- **Use active listening skills** by paraphrasing what customers are saying. Customer service reps should also use open gestures that show signs of agreement, such as nodding, and display signs of interest and concern by a tilt of the head.
- **Avoid the appearance of being cold and uncaring.** Applying active listening skills involves requesting customers' active input into the solution finding process and in conversations. This demonstrates that their intelligence and experience are fully recognized.
- **Use first names of customers as often as possible**, in a way that sounds natural and not overused. Most people react favorably to hearing the sound of their own names.

POINTS TO PONDER — SOMETHING TO THINK ABOUT

1. What techniques do you employ to practice good communication skills? Explain.
2. What additional communication techniques can you add to the list mentioned within this lesson?

TRAINING ACTIVITY — APPLICATION & ACTION PLAN

For one week, after each customer encounter, analyze your service experiences and determine how well you are:

- Explaining various concepts and thoughts
- Paying attention to the amount of time you speak
- Applying the tone and pattern of your speech
- Displaying enthusiasm in your voice

1. Identify areas where you need to improve.
2. Practice until you have polished the weaker areas that cause you to be more ineffective.

8

Listening Is Part of the Communication Process

Listening and active communication is a complex process where individuals use verbal and nonverbal symbols to share meanings and impart information. It is a circular process that requires the interaction of two or more individuals, which is irreversible in nature. Once a particular message is communicated, it cannot be recalled or altered.

Service representatives should understand that because of the complexity of communication, information often becomes garbled. Messages can be easily misdirected, incorrectly implied, or misinterpreted. Unless clarified, one communication problem creates another, increasingly escalating more problems to contend with.

IMPLICATIONS — WHAT THIS MEANS TO YOU

Active communication involves a series of actions that results in the transmission of information between individuals. It is a series of exchanges between people. Before communication can continue, the speaker must receive a response from the listener. These responses can include spoken words, silence or gestures that convey some form of a reaction to what was said. On-going communication continues as both the sender and receiver transmit and interpret various messages from one another. Therefore communication is a circular process.

Each person within the exchange process is responsible for the success of the communication procedure.

This is important for service representatives to understand. The complexity of communication in the real world means that no individuals are capable of effectively communicating all of the time. The varying backgrounds of people, their attitudes, experiences, values, beliefs, communication skills and a host of other factors directly impact how they listen to and interpret the messages that are sent to them. This is applicable to both customers and service representatives. Neither is immune from communication problems. Every act of communication is as unique as the people involved. This is why service representatives must treat each customer exchange as being unique unto itself, no matter how often they have heard similar problems, issues or concerns expressed to them before.

STRATEGIES, TIPS & TECHNIQUES TO APPLY

Communication is an ongoing process of exchanging and managing information. Since communication is dynamic, both the sender and receiver need to respond readily and appropriately for the process to be successful. The ability and capability of both parties to listen is the foundation of successful communication. An examination of the communication process demonstrates the importance of listening.

Gathering Information

The ability of individuals to competently gather information is the initial step in effective communication. They must be able to use all of their senses to gather information. This is normally encapsulated in what is considered to be proactive listening. People hear what other people are saying by listening, but this goes beyond the words that are being stated. It is how words are positioned, phrased, defined, or emphasized etc., and the tone of the voice that defines the attitudes and posture of the speaker. Pauses, sighs and other nonverbal cues are also inherent in active communication.

When dealing with customers in person, there are a number of additional nonverbal cues that assist in communication, including facial expressions, body posture and gestures. All of these contribute to the messages that are being communicated, which help service representatives to receive and gather appropriate and complete information.

Encoding and Decoding Information

When individuals encode and decode information, they begin processing the data that has been gathered and subsequently transform it into usable information. As information is gathered through the senses, the senders encode the information or transform it into meaningful symbols or codes. This is the language senders use to communicate. The initial information being sent has no direct or implied meaning. Specific meaning is determined through the various symbols or codes, or the language that is directly applied to the imparted information. When senders use language that is familiar to the receivers, the chances of being clearly understood are enhanced. This also increases if the receivers have well-developed language skills and broad experiences.

Because words and gestures have no meaning until individuals apply significance to them, decoding must take place in order to interpret the messages communicated. The information gathered is often filtered through individual experiences, interests, responsibilities and concerns, which influences individual perspectives. These influences can bias the interpretations of the information and are often the basis of most communication problems. Individuals may correctly listen and hear what is being said, but inaccurately interpret it.

Storing Information

After messages are exchanged and decoded, both senders and receivers store their impressions of the exchanges into their memories. Receivers will remember the information conveyed by senders, including facts, perceptions, opinions and any other factors surrounding their exchanges. Senders will remember intents, contents of the messages and the reactions of the receivers. These memories tend to shape future communications between the involved individuals.

Processing Information

Individuals process information by making associations between new information they receive and the information already stored in their memories. Individuals process information in three ways:

Words, Numbers and Visual Cues – Individuals often classify stored memories by certain key words or concepts. A word, number or concept can trigger them to recall detailed and complex memories and ideas. This is why service representatives are capable of triggering potentially hostile responses from customers with a simple word or phrase without realizing what they are doing. A single word can trigger an entire series of related memories and ideas.

Physical and Emotional Responses – Often information is linked in individuals' memories to physical and emotional reactions. When someone has suffered traumatic, frustrating or highly anxious experiences, a simple word not only triggers their memory, but also the physical and emotional responses attached to it. Often individuals have little control over these responses. The hazard when dealing with certain customers is that service representatives end up walking into emotional minefields that are difficult to get out of.

Labeling – Individuals' beliefs and attitudes affect inward reactions and interpretations in regard to incoming messages. They also determine how messages are stored and processed. It is not uncommon for most people to make generalized comparisons that unfairly label other individuals with titles such as "ignorant," "naïve," "uncooperative," "hostile" or "angry."

POINTS TO PONDER — SOMETHING TO THINK ABOUT

1. Are you aware of how you tend to receive and interpret information?
2. Are you aware of your personal beliefs, values, attitudes and other factors that bias how you generally interpret information?

TRAINING ACTIVITY — APPLICATION & ACTION PLAN

Identify three or four personal or professional exchanges that you recently experienced, which you can easily recall.

1. Identify the specific factors or variables that you used to interpret the messages communicated to you.
2. Determine how you processed the information communicated to you using the following:
    - Words, Numbers and Visual Cues
    - Physical and Emotional Responses
    - Labeling
3. Identify the lessons you learned about yourself from this analysis.

About the Author

Timothy F. Bednarz, Ph.D. is CEO of the American Management Development Group, Inc. For over 20 years he has researched, designed and authored hundreds of learning and development programs used by Fortune 1000 companies.

He is also the author of *Great! What Makes Leaders Great. What They Did, How They Did It and What You Can Learn from It* (2011).

Speaking Availability

Timothy F. Bednarz, Ph.D. is available for speaking engagements for your next meeting or association event. He can be contacted at 800-654-4935 or by e-mail at timothy.bednarz@majorium.com.

Bulk Sales

Bulk sales of this book or any other titles available from Majorium Business Press. Inquiries can be directed to sales@majorium.com, or by phone at 800-6654-4935.

Quick Order Form

Fax orders: 715-342-1118. Send this form.

Telephone orders: Call 800-654-4935 toll-free. Have your credit card ready.

Email orders: sales@majorium.com

Postal orders: Majorium Business Press, 2025 Main Street, Stevens Point, WI 54481, USA.

Please send the following books:

____

____

____

____

Please send more FREE information on:

❑Catalog ❑Speaking/Seminars ❑Mailing Lists ❑Consulting

Name: ______________________________________

Address: ____________________________________

City: ____________________ State: _____ Zip: __________

Telephone: __________________________________

Email address: ________________________________

Sales tax: Please add 5.5% for products shipped to Wisconsin addresses.

Shipping by air:

United States: $4.00 for first book and $2.00 for each additional product.

International: $9.00 for first book; $5.00 for each additional product (estimate).

Made in the USA
Monee, IL
08 November 2026

67380780R00031